The Living God

Romano Guardini

The Living God

SOPHIA INSTITUTE PRESS®
Manchester, New Hampshire

The Living God was first published in Germany in 1930 under the title *Vom Lebendigen Gott* by Matthias Grünewald Verlag, Mainz. An English translation by Stanley Godman was published by Pantheon Books in New York in 1957. With slight emendations, the 1957 English translation is now published with the permission of Matthias Grünewald Verlag, Mainz, and Pantheon Books, New York.

Copyright © 1930 Matthias Grünewald Verlag, Mainz
(First edition, 1930; third paperback printing, 1991)
Alle Autorenrechte liegen bei der Katholischen Akademie in Bayern.

English translation Copyright © 1957 by Pantheon Books, Inc.
Copyright renewed 1985 by Random House, Inc. This translation
published by arrangement with Pantheon Books,
a Division of Random House, Inc.

Printed in the United States of America

All rights reserved

Jacket design by Joan Barger

The cover painting is a detail from *The Creation of Adam* by Michelangelo Buonarroti, in the Sistine Chapel, Vatican Palace, Vatican State (photo courtesy of Scala/Art Resource, New York).

Sophia Institute Press®
Box 5284, Manchester, NH 03108
1-800-888-9344

Nihil Obstat: Charles E. Diviney, *Censor Librorum*
Imprimatur: Edward P. Hoar, L.L.D., *Vicarius Capitularis*
Brooklyn, February 25, 1957

Library of Congress Cataloging-in-Publication Data

Guardini, Romano, 1885-1968.
    [Vom lebendigen Gott. English]
    The living God / Romano Guardini.
        p.   cm.
    Originally published: New York : Pantheon Books, 1957.
    ISBN 0-918477-49-2 (pbk. : alk. paper)
    1. God.   I. Title.
BT102.G7713   1997
231 — dc21   96-50905 CIP

98 99 00 01 10 9 8 7 6 5 4 3 2

Contents

Editor's Note: The biblical references in these pages are based on the Douay-Rheims edition of the Old and New Testaments. Quotations from some of the books of the Bible have been cross-referenced with the differing names and enumeration in the Revised Standard Version, using the following symbol: (RSV =).

The Living God

Introduction

The addresses that follow originated in the spoken word. They were not written in the study, but arose from the depth and joy of that relationship which exists between the preacher and the congregation that confides in him.

There is probably nothing more beautiful than this deep and gentle understanding between priest and people, and this very fact makes it all the more doubtful whether it is possible to transfer to print the words that are spoken out of such an understanding. Surely their most vital quality is likely to be destroyed.

Anyway, the reader will do justice to these addresses only if he is prepared and able to rescue them from the printed page and allow them to become living words again, living words addressed to him personally, although not only to him. As he reads these talks, which were originally spoken to a congregation, the reader may sometimes wonder of what relevance a particular point is to him personally, and he should remember that if he does find something that appears to contain no message for him, it may have been intended for someone else.

To read in this way is not always easy. We are too much accustomed to gliding over the surface of impersonal ideas and images. It needs a special effort to assimilate spoken rather than written words — to become a listener instead of a reader. To make their full impact, these talks should be read at the proper time. They demand the concentration of an open and quiet mind.

The reader must try to attend to the individual words without tying them down too rigidly to a hard-and-fast meaning. He must give them space to move around in and the freedom to withdraw from the argument. A living word is complete only when the last movement of the argument has given shape to the last line, which influences and determines all that has gone before. It must be free to acquire color from the context of the hour in which it is spoken, from the faces of those who hear it and the progress of the movement of ideas. The final meaning of the sentence that opens a genuinely spoken address is conditioned by the words with which it closes.

To remember these things when reading the spoken words is always necessary but especially so when the subject is like the one discussed in the talks that follow, the subject of the living God. These talks are not concerned primarily with things that can be expounded in simple theological terms, although such things will be included, of course, since they form the foundation of all thought about God and keep it in the proximity of reason and reality.

The special intention of these talks is different: they are concerned with the living God; with the things that hover around the cut-and-dried concepts of theology; with the things that "pass all understanding"[1] and are nevertheless so very close at hand, with the things that cannot be defined conceptually, which, while not inimical to the conceptual, are more than merely conceptual, are deeper, higher, more intimate, and more heartfelt.

It is especially important that the reader should become a listener in a case like this. He must give the word freedom to move. He must give words that have already been uttered a chance to acquire new meaning as the talk proceeds. He must allow a sentence in which thought seems to be baffled by the mystery of the living God, which "passes all understanding," to be called into

[1] Cf. Phil. 4:7.

question or even contradicted by another sentence, since there is often no other way of giving one's ideas the dynamic impulse that will take them beyond the limits of the purely conceptual.

The listener must concede to the single talk the right to deal with a particular aspect of the subject from a particular angle, discovering, emphasizing, overemphasizing, illuminating, and overilluminating it — and then be prepared for another talk to supplement and correct the one that preceded it. The genuine listener must even allow for what may appear to be a momentary perversity in the spoken word. If he keeps an open mind, however, and waits patiently until he is able to take in the meaning of the series as a whole, then perhaps what appeared a false argument at a first hearing may prove to have been its very hub.

∞

Some readers may think this is a lot of fuss to make about a few talks. But they were not spoken lightly, and the writer may be forgiven for being rather concerned that they should find real hearers who will approach them in the right spirit.

1

God reveals His face to us

If we tell a child the story contained in the book of Genesis about how God planted a garden in Paradise and gave it to man to cultivate, and how one day He walked in the garden in the late afternoon, "in the cool of the day," and called Adam, who answered, "Here am I,"[2] the child will certainly understand it. Why should God not take a walk in the garden He made and which was so beautiful? Why should He not call Adam, and why should Adam not answer Him? To the child, all this will seem perfectly natural and straightforward.

Childhood and early youth, however, are followed by the years when religious doubts and difficulties appear and faith possibly has to be won all over again: if the same story is told to a person at this stage of life, he may refuse to accept it and may deny that God is like this at all. At best he will consider it a story for children, not a serious and realistic expression of the nature of God.

[2] Cf. Gen. 2:8, 15; 3:8-10.

The Living God

Time passes. Man enters into life, holds his own at work and among other men, and works with mind and hand and heart. If he is told this story or any other of the same kind, such as the one describing how men built the tower and God came down to see what they were doing; how corruption grew on the earth and God repented having created man[3] — if one were to ask a man in life's maturity whether he understood such a story, he would probably reply, with full awareness of the import of what he was saying, "Yes, I understand it, and it is true."

Something happens as we pass from childhood to youth and from youth to maturity. The ideas we use to grasp the realities of faith are not cut-and-dried, not incapable of growth and change. They are alive, and life implies growth. Knowledge of the realities of faith enters the soul like a living seed, through the words spoken by our parents, the teaching received in school and church, and probably from other sources as well. This knowledge lives in the life of him who receives it: it works and grows. Like a growing seed, it absorbs nourishment from the materials of the inner and outer life, from the ideas we receive and the experiences we

[3] Gen. 11:4-5; 6:5-6.

undergo. From all this, there is formed the living pattern of a spiritual reality. The materials from which it is formed change, since the life they came from changes. The unchanging foundations of spiritual reality there-fore are constantly acquiring new expression and new shape from the constantly changing materials of daily life. This is a wonderful process.

We have spoken about the central constituent of this process: man's changing idea of God. God is the Eternal. His reality is one and never changes, but the process by which man conceives the truth of God is a profoundly living process and therefore is subject to change and growth.

For the child, God is "dear God": the highest of all beings. The child meets Him in his daily life, in the quiet places of the heart and possibly with greater purity and at a greater depth than the adult. The child takes the material for his conception of God from the highest that he knows and above all from his parents. God in Heaven is the mightiest and worthiest of all beings. He governs the world just as the child's father rules in his own professional sphere.

The world revolves around the child. Inner and outer things, matter and spirit, reality and fable are all interwoven. God has created this world, and it belongs to Him. He is its ruler, and He does what He wills, as the child's father does in his business and as his mother does in the home and as the child himself does with his toys and the creatures of his imagination. If one tells a child how God dealt with the first human beings, how He scolded them for their disobedience and turned them out of Paradise;[4] or if one tells the child how God grieved when He saw the desolation of man's life on earth, of the terrible punishment He inflicted on man and His subsequent repentance, and how, because man is so weak, God decided not to let him suffer so cruelly any longer and set the rainbow in the clouds as a token of His mercy[5] — all these and other similar stories from the Bible the child will understand, rightly divining their profoundly spiritual meaning.

But then a big change begins to take place. The child's world breaks up. There is a mighty stirring of new life. The desire for life beyond the bounds of childhood awakens and expands. There comes a longing for the infinite. The adolescent becomes critical of the narrow

[4] Gen. 3:16-19, 23.
[5] Gen. 6:6-7; 8:21; 9:13.

molds in which childhood's life was set; the immediate coherence and continuity of the child's world dissolve. The inner and outer worlds are no longer indivisible and interwoven. The youth faces the outside world and strives to acquire self-confidence; he tries to attain stability within and scope without. And the more insecure he feels, the more critical and sensitive he will be.

He has a sense of spiritual realities, of their supreme importance, and of his responsibility for them. The place where he senses the reality of the spiritual and passionately experiences its absoluteness is the very place where he senses the reality of his own personality. He struggles the more intolerantly against everything that appears to contradict the purity of the spiritual.

And so the struggle for God begins: the struggle for a conception of God that is such that the youth can believe in it intensely and, at the same time, one that has in it the whole wideness of life and that accords with the passion and maturity of the adult mind. He searches, usually quite unconsciously, for other bases and criteria for the idea of God. He feels that the infinite and the eternal, the spiritual reality and truth of God, are all-important. His sense of infinity and the seriousness of his young mind encourage this strong feeling. The universal validity of the natural law and the sublimity and severity of the moral law — laws that stand above all individual particularities — appear as worthy criteria for the idea of the God who rules in the universe as these laws rule in the life of the world and man. Again, God is He who permeates the universe as the human heart permeates the world. The depth of the stream of life, the power of enthusiasm, the yearning for infinity, and the great experience of love become symbols of the infinite.

At this stage of life there is a jealous regard for the purity of the idea of God, *purity* signifying that nothing that is mutable, finite, material, or bound by human limitations ought to be said of Him. God must exist in an immaculate and unchanging spiritual purity, in unrestricted infinity. When the Bible refers to Him as "traveling on the wings of the storm,"[6] this may well be a beautiful poetic simile, but if the question is whether it is to be taken seriously, intrinsically, a young man will deny it in astonishment, for how can God "travel"? How can God see men building the tower and come down to investigate what they are doing? How can He become

[6] Cf. Ps. 17:11 (RSV = Ps. 18:10).

angry and turn their language to confusion? After all, God is eternal mind, eternal truth, the all-fulfilling Infinite!

∞

Later on, though, another change occurs. The youthful sense of infinity abates. Man comes to realize his limitations. He begins to see the clear, hard outlines of things. He sees the illusion in the yearning for the infinite. At the same time, he comes to understand what "man" really is: man with all his limitations and in the clarity and sobriety of his awakened life. Man is so much more than infinity! When one man meets another and they understand one another and a communion of experience and honor is born, that is something incomparably higher than the coldly indifferent "natural law." When one person cares for another and enters into the other's troubles as though they were his own, what takes place is deeper than the operation of an abstract "moral law" in a lifeless vacuum. Character is greater than talent; personality is deeper than the immensity of nature; the finiteness that has been accepted and lived through, and fought through, is nobler than the illusory infinity of adolescent emotionalism.

The Living God

At this later stage of development man comes to see, too, that the adolescent idea of God was not definitive. A concern for the purity of the idea of God leads to spiritual rigidity, or to vagueness and elusiveness. Now a new certainty and precision enters in, and at the same time a new vitality: the decisive vitality of the personality. The ideas that God looks at and inclines to man, that He leads him and gives Himself to him, all acquire a new meaning. Man feels that he would willingly abandon the "spirituality" and immutability of the youthful conception of God for the spiritual depth of a new idea of God, in which more stress is laid on the apparently manlike nature of God, on His historicity as it appears in the Bible and which angers the "wise of this world."[7] Conscious that he is advancing to something far deeper and more fundamental, man now ventures on to the God with whom it is possible for man to speak and come to an understanding.

However, it is not in any sense a matter of losing something one had really possessed hitherto. The immutability and infinity of God remain, but a new element is added. It is as though before one had seen the

---

[7] Cf. 1 Cor. 1:27.

stars merely in the cool austerity of their interrelation-ships or the sea in the flowing of its uncontainable waves, and now a clear and living face emerges from them. All the previous aspects of God remain, but they are now conditioned by the fact that God is a personal-ity. He is no longer "the God of the philosophers" or "the God of the poets," but "the living God" of the Bible.[8]

There is even more to this most sublime of all stories of how the idea of the living God and man's relationship to Him are molded by the materials of our human life. But let us leave it there for the moment.

What the Bible understands by "the living God" far exceeds all we have described so far. The child's ideas, the youth's ideas of spirituality and infinity, the adult's experience of the depth and significance of personal relationships: all these are merely a preparation, a pre-sentiment. Revelation alone can lead us into the full reality of God. All we have said so far is merely a gateway and a guide to the real questions.

[8] Deut. 5:26; Ps. 41:3 (RSV = Ps. 42:2); Matt. 16:16.

2

*God's Providence
dwells in every event*

The idea of Providence constantly recurs in the New Testament and expresses the essence of what Christ brought to man. A number of Christ's sayings refer to it: the one about the sparrow not falling from the roof without the Father's knowledge;[9] about the birds He feeds and the flowers He clothes.[10] We are exhorted not to worry about food and drink;[11] to pray for bread today and tomorrow, entrusting the future to the Father's hands.[12] Again and again, the mystery of Providence is expressed in the words "your Father in Heaven."[13]

These sayings all imply that man's whole life and existence and everything that belongs to him is surrounded by an infinite goodness. Nothing that happens

[9] Cf. Matt. 10:29.
[10] Matt. 6:26, 30.
[11] Matt. 6:31.
[12] Matt. 6:11.
[13] Cf. Matt. 5:16.

is purely accidental; the whole course of things is guided by a loving concern for man's welfare.

We must not accept this too glibly. When we look around the world, it does not seem that things really work out quite like that. Events go on their relentless way — and how often they ignore the individual and his happiness! Good men pine away and are unable to exert their influence to the full: they might have done so much good with their life-giving hands. Creative men die before they have borne their fruit; others prosper seemingly unjustly. The defenseless are violated. Pure thoughts can find no scope for expression; precious things are destroyed, but inferior, mediocre, vulgar things thrive and flourish.

The world sometimes appears to be governed by senseless despotism and destructive chance. Sometimes it is as though a malicious spirit were at work destroying a thing of beauty just when it is on the point of blossoming, or a rare destiny at the moment it is about to be fulfilled.

Someone may reply that, nevertheless, order reigns supreme in the world, that everything is governed by exact laws. Certainly there is an order in the world. But it is not concerned with man. It goes its way regardless of him. Or is it in fact designed to promote human fulfillment, or social justice, on however modest a scale? Perhaps we should say "individual fulfillment" rather than "human fulfillment" in general, since the human race consists of single individuals. Fulfillment can mean only that the individual's heart's desire is fulfilled, his creative urge given full scope, and his yearning for greatness consummated. But the universe ignores him: it goes its own way. The animals are not concerned with our affairs. They are caught up in the necessities of their own existence. The trees ignore us even when we eat their fruit. They grow and perish. The mountains do not look at us. They simply exist.

And yet people talk about "Providence."

What is Providence?

Providence surely exists if it can be demonstrated that I, with my living personality, exist in an order that does not constrain me, as the atom is constrained by the natural law, that does not use me as the factory uses its workers, but is guided by my needs. Everything that happens has me in mind. The course of the world accords with the innermost needs of my nature.

If we look at the world intelligently and on the basis of our experience, the order that governs it seems cold and blind. *Providence* means, however, that there is a seeing mind behind everything that happens and that I am the object of its seeing. It means that provision is being made for what is good for me. It means that there are eyes in the world that see everything, from which nothing is hidden that may injure or benefit me. It means that "not a hair of my head shall fall"[14] without being noticed and assessed with regard to my welfare and salvation. It means that there is significance in everything that happens in the world, and there is a heart, a concern, and a power stronger than all the powers of the world, which is able to fulfill the purposes of its care for man.

It is not right to take the mystery of Providence too much for granted or to speak of it as a natural, slightly improbable, slightly sentimental order that governs the world. The idea of Providence is grounded on the whole audacity of a living faith.

To believe in Providence, to realize the living faith in Providence, means to transform one's whole conception of the world. It ceases to be the world of natural science. It becomes alive. But it does not become a

[14]Cf. Luke 21:18.

magic world in which strange things happen and which ceases to exist the moment we come to grips with stern reality. To believe in Providence, it is not necessary to abstract the harshness from the world. The world remains what it is. *Providence* implies that the world, with its natural facts and necessities, is not enclosed in itself, but lies in the hands of a power and serves a mind greater than itself. The laws of inert matter do not cease to apply once life takes hold of them any more than the laws of physical growth cease to apply when the human heart and mind are busy building up their world. They remain, but they serve a higher purpose. And once you discern this higher purpose, you realize the service these forces and laws perform for it. *Providence* means that everything in the world retains its own nature and reality, but serves a supreme purpose that transcends the world: the loving purpose of God.

But this love of God for His creatures whom He has made His children is alive like that of a human being for his dear ones. The love of a father for his child pursues him in all his developments, in all his fortunes, and in all his ever-changing activities and decisions. So too the love of God for man is alive and ever new. And the whole world is drawn into the orbit of God's constant care for man. It embraces the whole world, past and present, in every passing moment of its existence and activity.

And so the world is renewed in every moment of time. Every moment has only one existence. It has not existed before, and it will not come again. It springs from the eternity of God's love and takes all being and all that is and all that happens into itself for the sake of God's children. Everything that happens comes to me from God, from His love. It calls me. It challenges me. It is His will that I should live and act and grow in it and become the person it is His will that I should be. And the world is to be perfected into that which it can become only through man — that is, through me.

But isn't all this just a beautiful story?

Or is it something I can only "believe" in the desperate sense of the word, without ever having a chance to experience it?

No, it is a reality, and it is possible to have personal experience of it.

There is a way of coming to experience it as a reality, and it is a way that is constantly recurring: it is "the now."

It is possible to conceive the idea of Providence with the mind alone, purely theoretically, by arguing that God has created everything and that everything that happens fulfills His will. If the world appears to contradict this theory, it can be argued that the totality of the forces at work in the world is so varied and the texture of purposes so complex that we cannot penetrate it and that we can see through the tangle of human destinies still less and must console ourselves with the idea that what appears to be meaningless destruction may be serving an ultimate purpose. To believe this would be a great deal, but much more is possible.

Providence is a reality; and we must not merely conceive this reality theoretically: we must act upon it in our lives. . . . It is not easy to express what I mean. A piece of news arrives: something has happened. The web of things and events and claims closes in around us. It — the situation — but no, it is not an "it" at all! At the deepest level of our minds we know it is *He*!

You must not force yourself to believe this, but must merely face the facts. Listen carefully, be on the alert, and one day you will realize that He is looking at you, speaking to you, challenging you. And then you will enter into unity with Him and act out of this encounter, from this situation of being spoken to and challenged — and that is Providence! You will be not merely thinking, but acting. You will be open to God, and Providence will be present.

What does this mean? It means that Providence is not a ready-made machine but is created from the newness of the freedom of God and also from our small human freedom. Not just anywhere, but here. Not just at any time, but now. It is a mystery of the living God, and you will experience it to the extent that you surrender yourself to it, not letting it merely pass over you, but cooperating with it. You are being called. God is drawing you into the weft of His providential creation. You must realize in your conscience what is at stake. You must set to work with your hands. You must use your freedom. As a living person, you must stand within the living activity of God.

The mystery of Providence will not come alive so long as we only think of it intellectually. It will become a reality only when we act upon it. Then we shall become aware of the meaning of "the living God." Then we shall realize: this moment of time is new. This situation never existed before. It does not exist in a vacuum of the imagination, but within the whole structure of reality. Now you must act as you ought to act — but in freedom. It is God who acts. It is you who act — if I may put it like this with all the due humility of the creature — in agreement with Him. No, I take it back. He acts alone. And yet, when God alone is acting, only then are we really ourselves. And that is Providence.

3

God gazes on us lovingly

The twenty-second chapter of the book of Genesis contains the story of the most difficult hour in Abraham's life, when God tested him and required of him the sacrifice of his only son, for whom he had waited so long.

Abraham obeyed, in an obedience of faith and trust that sealed him forever in God's promise. But in the bitterest moment, the angel of God called him and released him from the awful test.[15]

"And Abraham called the place: 'God sees.' "[16]

When the darkness of the ordeal surrounded him, he must have felt that he was engulfed in blind darkness, alone in his hopeless affliction. But now the dark walls fell, and he realized that he had not been forsaken, but had been standing in the sight of God.

God is He who sees.

[15] Gen. 22:1-12.
[16] Cf. Gen. 22:14.

The Living God

What a mystery is the seeing of the living God!

Most things in the world are beyond my sight. They are too far away for me to see. The world is too vast for me to survey. It is too detailed for me to grasp. But God sees everything: deserts, mountains, abysses, the depths of the sea, and the earth; the sun, the stars, the inconceivable immensities of the universe, and the inconceivably microscopic structure of matter — He sees it all. Everything that is happening now, in all places, everything that has happened in all the innumerable hours of the past, and everything that happened before the coming of man and the birth of the human mind — He sees it all. His eye is open and sees everything. His sight is all-embracing and all-penetrating. But that is not the greatest thing about Him.

It is said in the Bible that man sees only the outward appearance, whereas God looks into the heart.[17] The profounder inaccessibilities begin with man.

Man is external and internal, and each aspect is involved in the other. Behind every human exterior there is an interior quality that determines the outer appearance and gives it its character. But can this interior

---

[17]Cf. 1 Kings 16:7 (RSV = 1 Sam. 16:7).

quality be grasped with the same certainty as the outer appearance?

A man may do something that is on the face of it an expression of friendliness, but inside he may harbor dislike or even hatred. Sometimes it is possible to feel this or to sense that there is something ambiguous and disturbing about the action. There are people, however, who have their facial expression so much under control that it is impossible to guess what is behind it.

God sees the character behind the outer appearance, behind the gesture, and behind the facial expression. No matter how strong the will that controls them and no matter how deceptive the features may be — and even when a completely deceitful nature governs them — in God's sight they are all utterly revealed.

What gives meaning to an action is the motive behind it. A man may appear to be doing a service to another, but in fact may be calculating the profit that will accrue to himself. He is not concerned with the other's welfare, only with his own advantage. He helps the other man, and if he were asked why, he would reply, "Because I have his well-being at heart." And he would not have lied because he really believes that is a fact. But it may suddenly occur to him that he was helping the other man because he wanted to be seen. Vanity was lurking behind his desire to help the other man. And even vanity may not have been the ultimate motive. Other very obscure and very strange motives may have been involved.

One motive can be hidden behind another or mingled with another. An action may be conditioned by a whole tissue of motives: repressions, inhibitions, and frustrations — successive layers of the strangest disguises, camouflages, and substitutions, which it is almost impossible to disentangle. The outer actions and appearances of a man develop from the inner depths. If one tries to dig down from one layer to another, he may still not reach the ultimate foundations of a man's behavior. The depths may be a bottomless abyss.

But God sees. He sees right through the tangled webs of human motives. He distinguishes between the real and the unreal, between the expression and the intention, between the mask and the original. The roots, the foundations, the origins: all lie open to His sight.

∞

Sometimes a man does something stupid, clumsy, or inexpedient. In fact, however, his intention was quite different: it only failed to come off. He would like to be able to say what he intended, but he can't find the right words. He would like to express his convictions, but his looks and gestures won't let him. Sometimes one knows exactly what ought to be said, and one wants to say it quite honestly, but the words simply refuse to come.

It is even possible to intend to do something and not know what it is. One feels a restless urge to do something, but the silence within becomes deeper than ever. Even the unspoken words can find no release. This kind of repression gives rise to a lot of suffering. It is the source of much of the wrong we do to one another.

But God is He who sees and hears: He hears even the things that are not expressed, even the things that are not yet aware of their own existence.

When the Bible wants to say that something has passed the final test of truth, it says that it exists "in the sight of God."[18] It stands in the sight of God, penetrated by Him to its very ground: He hears its innermost silence, and He confirms what it claims to be.

What things are "in the sight of God" is quite different from what they are "in the sight of man" or in their

[18]2 Cor. 4:2.

own sight. Everything that happens happens in the sight of God, and God is constantly judging everything that is and everything that happens. Everything is seen by Him, as a whole and in all its details, outwardly and inwardly; He sees its causes and its effects, its origins and its development.

From this point of view it is not difficult to understand the meaning of the "fear of God."[19] The "fear of God" means not only being disturbed by an immediate sense of His tremendous power: it means an awareness of being penetrated by His gaze, of standing under His holy, incorruptible judgment, and of being unable ever to withstand His scrutiny.

But is it not a terrible thing to be seen through like this? To stand the merciless brightness of His gaze?

In laboratories and hospitals, there are rooms completely white, with little furniture — and what little there is is made of glass — lit by intolerably bright lamps with no cranny of darkness to hide in. Is this our situation in the sight of God? Are we like the patient on the

[19]Gen. 20:11.

operating table under the doctor's merciless eyes? That would be frightful. But that is not our situation at all.

There are various ways of being seen. The seeing eye does not merely reflect what it sees; it also acts upon it. Seeing is a creative activity. It influences what it sees.

A man can look at another with a look that hardens the other's heart. A man can look at another with curiosity, with lust or malice, with a look that hurts and destroys, or with a look that forces the other to resist. A man can look at another with cold indifference, humiliating and degrading the other. A man can also look at another with reverence, and when that happens the other will be given freedom and opportunity to be himself. A man can look at another with kindness and goodness, with a look that encourages and loves, that opens up what is locked up inside the other, that awakens his powers and brings him to himself.

God is He who sees, but His seeing is an act of love. With His seeing, He embraces His creatures, affirms them, and encourages them, since He hates nothing that He has created. When He had created the world, He saw that "everything was very good."[20] He sees men's

[20] Cf. Gen. 1:31.

possibilities and calls men to use them. He sees the evil in the world and judges it; He sees human sin and passes sentence on it. His judgment penetrates to the roots, and nothing can be hidden from Him, but He Himself has told us that He is loving and merciful and forgiving and redeeming.

The love of God is creative and redemptive. It created the world out of nothing and re-created the world after it had fallen. His seeing is not the kind that merely looks at something: it is creative love; it is the power that enables things to be themselves and rescues them from degeneration and decay.

God turns His face to man and thereby gives Himself to man. By looking at me He enables me to be myself. The soul lives on the loving gaze of God: this is an infinitely deep and blessed mystery.

God is He who sees with the eyes of love, by whose seeing things are enabled to be themselves, by whose seeing I am enabled to be myself.

∞

There is nothing brighter than the eyes of God, nor is there anything more comforting. They are unyielding, but they are the source of hope.

To be seen by Him does not mean to be exposed to a merciless gaze, but to be enfolded in the deepest care. Human seeing often destroys the mystery of the other. God's seeing creates it.

We can do nothing better than press on into the sight of God. The more deeply we understand what God is, the more fervently we shall want to be seen by Him. We are seen by Him whether we want to be or not. The difference is whether we try to elude His sight, or strive to enter into it, understanding the meaning of His gaze, coming to terms with it, and desiring that His will be done.

We can do nothing better than place ourselves and all that we have in God's sight: "Behold me!" Let us put away the fear that prevents us. Let us abandon the sloth, the pretense of independence, and the pride. "Look at the good! Look at the shortcomings! The ugly, the unjust, the evil, the wicked, everything — look at it, O God!"

Sometimes it is impossible to alter something or other. But let Him see it at any rate. Sometimes one cannot honestly repent. But let Him see that we cannot yet repent. None of the shortcomings and evil in our lives are fatal so long as they confront His gaze. The very act of placing ourselves in His sight is the beginning of renewal. Everything is possible so long as we begin with God. But everything is in danger once we refuse to place ourselves and our lives in His sight.

4

*God's will is
living and creative*

One day Jesus' disciples came to their Master and said, "Lord, teach us how to pray, as John did for his disciples."[21] A significant moment: Jesus was asked to tell them how to do the most intimate and the greatest thing possible, how to come to God, how to receive the things that come from God and to take to Him the things of man. He was to show them what they were to pray for and the state of mind in which they should pray.

So He taught them the Our Father. It is not simply one prayer among many, but the basic pattern of all Christian prayer, the embodiment of all the objects of prayer, and the expression of the attitude of mind that should condition all prayer.

This prayer contains a strange clause: "Thy will be done." Have you ever tried to realize fully what that means?

[21] Cf. Luke 11:1.

The Living God

∞

To begin with, it obviously means that the will of the Father is great and precious, something we are to desire in the earnest act of prayer. That is sufficiently remarkable in itself. We are not in the habit of regarding as precious the will of God that confronts us so gravely and often so troublesomely and admonishingly.

But one is even more amazed by the further consideration that arises from this clause: I am to pray that the will of God may be done; it is therefore possible for it not to be done! Isn't God almighty? Isn't His will a reality? And yet here I am asked to pray that His will may be done! What a strange concern this is in which I am called to share: to help see that the will of God is done. Is His will so frail and in danger of not being fulfilled?

The whole affair seems even more astonishing when one reflects that His will is apparently so precious and so exposed to danger that God Himself, the strongest power there is, is called upon to see that His own will is done. Man prays to God that His will may be done. Isn't that curious? This clause in the Lord's Prayer reveals a whole pattern of reality that implies that the will of God is both glorious and frail at the same time: it reveals the weakness of the will of God in the world and the fact that it is entrusted to the care of man. Yet this same man prays to God for help, and so his concern enters into cooperation with the victorious omnipotence of God, who is the Lord. Do you now sense the mystery of the living God?

∞

What is this will of God?

We have become far too accustomed to thinking of it in purely moral terms, as the sum total of our obligations, as a kind of personification of the "moral law." It is in fact much more than that. The will of God is simply what ought to happen in the world He has created, what ought to emerge from the interplay of natural forces, and what ought to emerge from man's work, from the freedom of the human spirit, so that the world may come to be what God intended it to be. The will of God is the consummation of the divine creation of which man, with his freedom, is part.

This is in itself inconceivably great. But there is more to it than that: the will of God is what God demands of man; in other words, what He requires of me. It is His will for me, for this one individual me, as a member of the total human race, and His will for the world through me.

But there is still more to be said. This will of God does not stand "over" me, "in front of" me, and say, "You must do this and that. You must become this sort of person." God does not give me marching orders. He is a living power ruling within me. The will of God is not merely a claim on me; it is also an active force. It is the special way in which He admonishes, urges, helps, sustains, acts, molds, struggles, overcomes, and perfects — inside me.

The will of God is the power with which He helps me to fulfill His demands. Seen in this light, it has another name: it is the power we call grace. When the will of God is done, it is the gift and achievement of this will itself. It is my work, but mine only through His, His will acting in me, the whole process being a mysterious unity.

It is possible to go even further: God's will is not ready-made within me, but something that is constantly being renewed and making ever-new demands on me. When I confront a duty and fail to fulfill it, the will of God has not been done. Does that imply the end of the will of God? Does God thereby cease to have a will for me? No, for at once He says again, "Do this." Admittedly a change has come over His will. The wrong has been done. It was not in accordance with His will, but once it has been done, His will — eternally the one, same, but living and ever-creative will of God — surrounds me as the doer of the wrong that leaves its mark within and its trail of consequences without. It is sin in the sight of God, but now He says, "Do this!" In other words, the will of God is not cut-and-dried once and for all, but encompasses my freedom and my activities and develops afresh from each new situation.

There is something relentless about all this. Nothing is forgotten. Nothing is overlooked. What is, is. It is all taken up into the demanding will of God and has to be endured.

But there is an ineffable wideness about it, too. There is always a will of God. There is always a way. When an officer is given an order and carries it out wrongly, the matter is finished. The order was what it was and has been wasted because it was not carried out properly. There is no way out. But there is always a way in the sight of God. Whatever may happen, good or evil, God passes judgment on it; but at the same time, He takes up what has happened and calls me to take the next step. And so the way continues. It may become harder and require more self-denial. It may be a way oppressed with a sense of guilt and loss; but it is a way all the same. It is not a way marked out in advance, but a way that God prepares under man's very feet, that He creates anew from every step we take.

This will of God is the love of the Father. It is not an impersonal law, but the living, creative power of the Creator of man and the world. It is not a command issued by a sovereign to his subjects, but the personal claim of a Father on His sons and daughters. It is His loving will for the individual child of God, a living force that encourages and sustains. It is the gracious act of love that enables the claim to be heard and affords the power to fulfill it. It is the power of the love that gives all; it is being, power, and deed.

The things that arise from this power become part of me. This is the understanding that the Almighty has with freedom, the secret of which is that the stronger the power of grace, the more freely freedom belongs to itself. He makes no rigid demands. His love is eternally renewed, guided by a Father's constant care for His children. God accompanies everything that happens, cooperating with human freedom. This is the ineffable mystery of His patience, which is possible only because He is the truly living God and the almighty living God.

∞

And now we may have come to see why we are taught to pray that "God's will be done." The fact is that the more profoundly a man has become a Christian, the more alive will be his concern to do the will of God and the more aware he will be that this will is the most precious and the most gentle and the most powerful thing in the world. And the more he realizes his own wretchedness and untrustworthiness, the more he will turn to the Lord of the world and pray that he may cherish and fulfill that high purpose on which the meaning of everything depends. At the same time, he will grow more confident that the will of God will be done and will triumph over all the powers of evil.

The Christian carries deep within him the fear that he may decline from God's holy will; the anxiety that he may deface the beauty of His will, that he may lose sight of His irretrievable purpose. And so he prays for the patience of God. Yet he tells himself that it is impossible for God's will to be lost. Sin appeared to have destroyed God's will for the world, but it was followed by the tremendous fact of redemption. The creation that had been destroyed was taken up into the hope of a "new Heaven and a new earth."[22]

But the Christian may not deduce safe guarantees from this. In the constant, absorbing care that God's will may be done, he must persevere and watch and work.

[22]Rev. 21:1.

5

Our repentance addresses
the living God Himself

When Moses was called by God as he kept the flocks of Jethro on Mount Horeb, he saw a bush in flames, yet the bush was not consumed. He wanted to investigate, but he heard a voice saying, "Draw not nigh hither: put off thy shoes from thy feet, for the place whereon thou standest is holy ground."[23] We have ventured to meditate on the nature of Him whom the Bible calls the living God, and we have already heard the call: "Put off thy shoes from thy feet." The shoes we use in other places refuse to take us any further here. They take us up to a certain point; then we must put them off our feet. Yet this is the point where the real mystery begins, the mystery in which the deepest thing within us, the heart, begins to feel at home.

The organ by which we obtain our deepest knowledge of God is, in biblical language, the heart. The mind has its part to play in the knowledge of God: a good task

[23] Exod. 3:1-5.

The Living God

and a clear one set by the Creator Himself. But when it has done its task and cannot go any further, it realizes that it cannot get any further because it is being superseded by something greater than itself. If at this point the heart feels that it has attained to reality, then we stand before the living God. One of the places where the bush burns with fire is the place of repentance.

A child has done something he ought not to have done. His mother sees what he has done and scolds the child. His own feeling and the mother's words coincide: the child realizes he has done wrong, and he is sorry. But once the sorrow has been overcome and the mother says, "I forgive you," the child is comforted. The mother then teaches the child that God has seen the wrong he has done, and she tells him that he has done wrong in the sight of God, not merely in her own sight. The child's sorrow for what he has done is now directed to the loving and stern God, who is angry with the child. The mother says, "If you make up your mind not to do it again, God will forgive you." Again the child is comforted, but at a deeper level. He senses the mystery that is at work here.

Now imagine someone who has worked his way through the questions of which we have already spoken. This person has done wrong. It oppresses him, and someone he discusses it with, who is able to talk to him like this, tells him that God forgives the sin that is brought to him in repentance. Such a person may easily be surprised and ask himself, "What does this mean — 'God forgives'?"

Once a man has realized the significance of "Thou shalt," once he has sensed the dignity and relentlessness of the moral law, the idea of God's forgiveness may well appear quite absurd, almost a betrayal of the sovereignty and sublimity of the moral law. There have been thinkers in whom this feeling was very strong, and this explains the power they have had over very serious and morally austere minds. Immanuel Kant,[24] for example, was so immensely impressed by the majesty of the ethical demand "Thou shalt" that he paid no heed to anything else. For him it was the greatest thing of all. Moral activity and the bearing of responsibility were an ultimate for him beyond which there was nothing at all, not even divine forgiveness.

[24]Immanuel Kant (1724-1804), German philosopher.

There is a lot of truth in this objection. It comes from the deepest level of conscience, and it would be wrong to cover it up with pious words of consolation. We have already said that religious folk are all too prone to jump from wrongdoing to the solace of forgiveness and feel themselves far too quickly absolved from the stain of wrongdoing.

It is in fact possible for the idea of forgiveness to soften the relentlessness of the moral order and lessen the weight of conscience, although if it has that effect, it will itself be corrupt, since real forgiveness contains within itself the whole severity of the moral law.

In purely "ethical" terms, the point is that when I have done something, I have done it. It exists for all eternity. It cannot be wiped away. To begin with, forgiveness has no meaning within this situation. There is nothing for it to base itself on. It is overpowered by the relentlessness of the moral law. Speaking purely ethically, that is, from the basic experience of finding myself confronted with the imperative "Thou shalt" and its absolute demands, it must be said that the wrong I have done has been done, its reality is indelible, and I am bound to answer for it. It is my duty to realize what I have done, and I must endeavor not to do it again, but it still has a reality of its own: it has not been extinguished. In the same way, any good I have done continues to exist and is just as far removed from the influence of all that may come afterward. There is a sublimity about the stern reality of good and evil. It is the source of what we call "character."

What do we mean when we say, "God forgives"? We certainly do not mean that He says, "Never mind. Try to do better in the future!" or, "Don't worry. Cheer up! I am not going to take it as seriously as all that." That would be quite unworthy, and the wrong would remain. We mean something far greater. We mean that the sin no longer exists in truth and reality and in the sight of my conscience.

The moral law is not above God, supervising and controlling even His actions. The moral law that binds us is not an abstract law, but the living God. What He does, the moral law itself does. This is the source of God's own ultimate sovereignty: the moral law itself speaks when He speaks.

But the mystery is still deeper. It is as incredible as the mystery that the world arose from nothing. It is beyond human imagination how God created the world from nothing. And here, too, the mystery is that God creates, that God draws man — with all that he has done — to Himself, draws him into His ineffable power over being and nonbeing.

Still more, He draws him into the mystery of the power that it would be a violation of the majesty of the moral law to conceive as belonging to anyone but God; He draws man into the mystery of His power not only to give life to the nonexistent, but to call the guilty to new innocence. A new creation takes place. God draws man to Himself with all that man has done; He draws him into His ineffable power, and man comes forth again renewed and guiltless. There is no need for God to avert His eyes from the sin: it no longer exists. Conscience does not need to look away from sin: it no longer exists.

He who is able to do this, who not only says this but enables it to be done, does not infringe upon the majesty of the moral law like a despot overriding right and wrong. Rather, by so doing He in fact fulfills the moral law: for He is the living God. He is not merely the supreme guardian of the moral law, as conceived by Kant, providing an assurance that sometime or other the moral order will coincide with the order of bliss: He is the living God, who is able to forgive.

Our repentance addresses God

∞

But what about the gravity of sin?

We have left something out of account: repentance. So long as we keep merely to the "ethical," there is no place for repentance. Real repentance will have no place in the life of a person whose life is based solely on the rigid moral law and the binding force of conscience. Such a person believes that he must accept the consequences of what he has done. He cannot allow anyone to relieve him of the burden of guilt. He does not in fact want to be relieved of it, for that would destroy the true worth of his personality. He wants to bear the consequences; he wants to reform himself; but what has already happened still remains. There is something in-human about this attitude, but at the same time a sublime consistency. Repentance belongs in the sphere of the living God.

∞

What is repentance? It not only means that a person realizes he has done wrong, wishes it had not happened, is prepared to bear the consequences, and is determined to make amends. Repentance is more than that. Repentance is an appeal to the living God. He is the Holy

The Living God

One, unapproachable and intolerant of all wrongdoing. At the same time, however, He is love and He is the Creator who has the power not only to bring man to life, but also to bring him to something inconceivably higher still: He has the power to re-create and purify the personality burdened and defiled by sin.

Repentance is an appeal to the deepest mystery of the creative power of God. The merely "ethical" is swallowed up in the ineffable life of the Holy One. Repentance does not cover up sin. On the contrary, repentance is truth. It tries to see things as they really are. The forbidding and frightening element in sin has no part in repentance. Fear is a byproduct of sin and can only confuse genuine repentance. Repentance seeks to know the truth. And with the truth of what he has done, man comes to God and says: "I am guilty before Thee. I admit it. Thou art the judge. I come before Thee, against myself. I desire Thee. I want Thy will to be done, for Thou art holy. Thou art in the right against me. I love Thee. I judge myself as Thou judgest me. But Thou art love, and I appeal to this love. With all that I am, I give myself to the mystery of Thy love. I have no desire to evade the severity of Thy judgment. But Thou art the God of grace!" These things are beyond the power of the mind to understand. But the heart understands and knows.

Human repentance corresponds to divine forgiveness. To the living God who is able to forgive, there corresponds the man of living faith who is able to repent. Both constitute a single mystery of holy life.

Repentance is itself a gift. When man comes to God with his repentance, the living God is already in him and has given him repentance. Something has not been merely covered up: I have been born again. I begin again.

This is a deep mystery, but our hearts tell us that it is the living God who makes it possible.[25]

[25] There may be an overemphasis in all this. The ethical may, perhaps, not be conceived as "purely ethical." The ethical implies the living person and its love, and hence a premonition of repentance. Let us, however, try to penetrate to the depth of what has been said, and we will realize the awesome quality of the concept of forgiveness.

6

God speaks to our hearts

The Bible expresses the depths of the living God in various ways. There are certain sayings that summon us to apply our intellectual faculties to them. As we penetrate them layer by layer, His mystery and His power come before our minds. But there are other sayings whose real meaning lies beyond the limits of conceptual thought. The real depth that speaks to us in them comes from another source.

We have already said that God is He who sees. We have tried to penetrate the mystery of this divine seeing. We have seen its greatness and felt its depth and sensed in it something of the meaning of God's inner life. We shall have a similar experience if we try to penetrate one of the most beautiful sayings in the Bible, in the twentieth verse of the third chapter of the first letter of John: "If our heart condemns us, God is greater than our heart, and knoweth all things."

The saying is inscrutable. But its depth does not come from the intellectual sphere. It speaks of the "condemnation of the heart." This means more than that the mind says to us, "You have done wrong," or that conscience reproaches us and says, "You have done wrong." No, the heart condemns us, and that is more. From the condemnation of the mind come the painful insights of reason. From the condemnation of conscience comes the bitter conviction of guilt. Both lay a burden on man. But from the condemnation of the heart, there comes something more: something that affects us in quite a different way; something that hurts us quite differently; something that gives rise to quite a different kind of sorrow.

The condemnation of the heart comes from far away. The distance from which it comes is beyond measure. It comes from the very roots of life. There is a kind of wrong to which a name can be given, but from this wrong there emerges something that is impossible to put into words. Life itself condemns us. Life reproaches us with having wronged life itself. There may be sorrow for the failures of our youth in this accusation, the painful sense of having lost something that can never be made up for, the grief of the love that has not been fulfilled, and the deeply oppressive sorrow that life with its yearning for infinity passes by so unspeakably quickly. The sin that the heart condemns is deep-seated. It implies that we have not merely done wrong in the ethical sense, but that we have sinned against life itself. It has a depth and a grief far greater than any other.

Reason may assert itself and say, "What I did was right after all, for this or that reason. What I did had to be." Conscience may defend itself and say, "Anyway, my intentions were good." But such excuses avail nothing here. The condemnation of the heart comes from a source beyond the reach of this kind of defense. Yet we have still left the basic thing unsaid.

In the condemnation of the heart, it is God Himself who condemns. Wrong has been done to *Him*. Wrong has been done to the gentle and holy life that He has awakened in the heart, to the holy trust that binds Him to His child. How can man's self-defense reach these depths?

What possible help is there? John says, "If our heart condemns us, God is greater than our heart." Do you observe that this answer comes from the same depths as the condemnation itself? The answer is not: "You have done right. Your intentions were good. Be of good cheer." No, the answer is: "God is greater than your heart."

The Living God

Your heart is great. That is the first thing, and it is amazing that that should be said at all. But God is still greater. The heart that has been lost is great. But God is greater. The heaviness of the heart to which wrong has been done is so great that it must sink. God is the sea of greatness where everything heavy is made light. The wrong that has been done to life is great. God is the Creator, and God is life and grace. He is greater than everything. The holiness to which wrong has been done partakes of the dignity of God. His trust has been infringed. That is terrible. But He Himself, His magnanimity, His creative love, is greater than all this wrong. John does not say, "Cheer up, it isn't so bad after all." He does not say, "Don't take life so seriously." God says, "Give these things their full weight. Then I will come to you. I am God."

And when He comes, the creature will become clear to itself. Its self-importance will be dissolved, and everything will be fulfilled.

John's saying is ineffably profound. Its depth is not an intellectual depth. It comes from another source. It is immeasurable and therefore forever new. Let us meditate on these lines again: "If our heart condemns us, God is greater than our heart" — and then what do we expect to follow: "and will console it" or "and will assuage our suffering"? No, what follows are the words "and knoweth all things."

This knowledge has the brightness of the sun and sets everything in the full truth of its existence. This knowledge has the depth of the sea in which everything sinks. It has the infinite embrace of the love in which everything is redeemed.

Each one of these sentences is deep. The thought behind them goes on and on and comes to no end. But the deepest thing of all is the relationship between the three clauses. That is something in which the mystery of God itself speaks in its original tongue.

It may be said — insofar as there is any desire to say anything at all and not rather simply to listen in the quietest place of the heart — that there is an answer to every real and every live question, which is that God is God. That is the final answer, faith's most authentic answer.

All the less-than-ultimate answers say: "This is so because that was so. This is happening because it is the outcome of that. This must be so because it is necessary for this or that purpose." Such answers are good in themselves, but each of them raises a new question.

The Living God

There is only one answer that, provided it is really given, answers every question because it puts an end to all questioning: the answer that He is who He is.[26] May He grant us to know who He is.

[26]Cf. Exod. 3:14.

7

*God loves us
with abiding patience*

There are deep words in human speech. They enshrine insights into the very nature of things, into the fundamental patterns of life, and not merely insights, but experiences. What they contain are not simply facts that have been recorded, but things that have been seen; not only life that has been observed, but life that has been lived. Some of these words have a depth all their own: the names man has given to God.

To some extent we have received them from God Himself; they are revelations by which He tells us who He is and how we are to address Him. But as the nature of man rests in God and man becomes truly man by adhering to God, the names of God also contain revelations about man.

The fact that God has been called "the one who sees" means that men of vision have felt themselves seen by God. They have felt His gaze penetrating their very being so that it lay before Him like an open book. They have recognized Him as Him before whose eyes there are no walls. They have learned that man stands in the sight of God as in the light. They have learned that God's seeing eye judges and creates at the same time, that it is both terrible and redemptive. In chapter 3, we spoke of the story told in the book of Genesis in which Abraham uses the phrase "God sees" to express the infinite relief of his heart when he receives his son back from the altar.[27] And in Psalm 138,[28] the psalmist finds unspeakable comfort in the thought that wherever he may go, God's all-seeing eye will penetrate him still. God is the seer, man the seen.

Other names for God have arisen from the human heart itself, taught by God, who has given them to the heart. Let me speak of one such name here, one that comes from a very deep, heartfelt experience, the one that calls Him the Lord of Patience.

The mystery of the divine patience is very deep. What does it mean?

In order to answer that question, we must first ask what it is that He is patient with. The reply is that He is patient with the creation; with us men as part of

[27]Cf. Gen. 22:14.
[28]RSV = Ps. 139.

creation; and with me as a man among men: that is the true answer.

When God created the world, He did not finish it as a man finishes making an instrument, which is completed once and for all and merely needs to be kept in working order. God intended that the world should be completed in long, immeasurably long, periods of time. But God's patience is the power with which He encompasses what are experienced by us as inconceivably broad expanses of time, and uses them to achieve His purposes.

When we were children, our mother may have given us a potted plant. When the buds came, we could not wait for them to open by themselves. We tried to force them. We took away the outer petals to try to make the buds open more quickly. The result was that they withered and died. That is man's way with life. His time is running out. He wants things to happen quickly. But God has time. He is above all time. He is eternal. Eternity is the mode of God's existence. He creates time. Time is the mode of created existence. God can therefore wait until the time is ripe — the time He Himself has appointed. Man wants everything straightaway; God knows that one thing can come only after

The Living God

the other. He therefore allows things to develop quietly, freely, each thing in its own good time. A scientist can tell you how old the mountains are; how long the basalt took to come from the earth's interior in a glowing effusion to solidify into the gigantic shapes of the mountains. He can tell you how long life needed to evolve through its gradually developing formations. God encompasses all this in the quiet calm of His eternity. He has patience.

God has made the world so that things do not exist all together, but each in its own self and each in its own time, and only when the preconditions for its emergence have been fulfilled. Each has its own time and place in the coherent pattern of life.

Wisdom is knowledge of the time that belongs to things. Some people never learn it. Some learn it very late. Hardly anyone learns it completely, since man is involved in disorder and disorder gives rise to impatience. Man wants things to suit his own convenience, and then they are spoiled. A book takes his fancy; he pounces on it, but he is not prepared for it, and either it has no influence on him at all or its influence is harmful. A thought suddenly occurs to him, and he tries to force others to share it; but the preconditions for its acceptance have not yet appeared, and he only causes confusion. He has an urge to do something, but he does not give the plan time to mature; he fails to make the right preparations; he does not shape his plans consistently, so that the result is only half finished and lacks permanence and stability. Wisdom and patience are one and the same thing. Man has neither, fully.

The nature of God is as simple as light, and yet it contains the fullness of all possibilities. He Himself is living, holy, and wise. He rejoices that everything has its own time and place. He has the great creative patience that brings things to fulfillment.

In the world that God has created, there are human beings, and in this human world, there is freedom. But this freedom is in the hands of a being that can err. Freedom can therefore degenerate into evil and folly. This has happened. Man has sinned.

Among the first acts of man were disobedience, rebellion, and impatience. He wanted to be like God. He had been created in the image of God and was intended for a life of fellowship with God, "to share in the divine nature."[29] In the fullness of time he would

[29] Cf. 2 Pet. 1:4.

have been "like God,"[30] after a period of probation and through divine grace. But he wanted to be like God straightaway and through his own efforts and in his own right. So he lost what he already was and fell below his own proper level. The result is the existence of sin in the world, which destroys the work of God.

What would man have done if what he has done to God had been done to him? He would probably have acted like the gods he has created in his own image: he would have hurled the evildoer down into ruin. Praise be to God that He is not as man imagines Him to be!

The meaning of God's patience is fully revealed only when He is seen to be using it with man. He has never allowed man to escape from His love for a single moment. He has held him fast. He has promised him redemption. Over long — infinitely long — periods of time, He has allowed the human race to taste to the full the sin it has committed in order to prepare it for conversion. He has sent His messengers to admonish and prepare it until in the fullness of time the Son of God became man and brought the infinite possibilities of the kingdom of God.

[30]Gen. 3:5.

God loves us with patience

Man's answer was the second fall. The light was in the world, and the world received it not.[31] Once again, God was not seized with anger. He did not allow the world to perish, but from the very sufferings that the world inflicted on His Son, He created the work of redemption. Christ continues to live in the world. He acts in the world. He struggles desperately for the hearts of men. But again the will of man has become entangled with God's holy will. God holds fast. With indomitable patience He continues to act through time.

How would a man deal with men if the living truth were in the world and they were always betraying it? His own evil would rise up within him and rage against the evildoer. He would hate his own blind, indignant soul in the other and would fly out at it. He would certainly have no patience.

Man is a sinner, and that is why he has no patience. Sin is impotence and violence at one and the same time. God is pure. He is strong. Therefore He can be gentle. He can see evil being done and can condemn it and still remain calm. He can even see the good spark in evil and have a concern for it. God's goodness is His patience.

[31] Cf. John 1:9-11.

The Living God

Human beings cannot even order their own work or their own lives. From the very beginning, human life is beset with flaws and blemishes. Deep insights are bound up with errors and run aground. Enterprises that ought to mature over a long period lose their roots and wither. An undertaking apparently blessed with the prospect of success develops hopefully and is then thwarted by some malignant accident, and the whole enterprise comes to naught. Human relationships are so muddled that we all seem to be living in spite of, rather than with, our fellows. Human friendships are hardly ever a complete success. Love is hardly ever perfectly fulfilled.

God is not indifferent to these things. He did not create the world and the human race for men to play about in it like children on a heap of sand, not caring what they make of it, so long as they behave themselves. The works of man continue the work of creation in the realm of freedom. What takes place in the world of nature is governed by natural laws. But spiritual, moral, and social values can arise only from freedom. These things have been left to man, and it is his task to bring them to fruition. That is God's will.

Man is not merely to behave well and for the rest, to do exactly what he likes: he is to do his work properly.

God loves us with patience

That is the first moral test that God imposes on him. Man is called to follow the good life, to administer God's creation aright, and to develop the work begun by God. But look at how man treats God's world. He rapes and ruins it.

God sees the chaos that man has created, but He does not lose His patience. What does a master do if his apprentice is always ruining his tools and materials? He berates and punishes him, and one day he turns him out altogether. He cannot afford to have inexhaustible patience, since he is weak and his means are limited. But God is almighty and infinitely rich. His riches and His omnipotence are His patience. How good it is that God's patience is as great as His omnipotence! That is why He is always able to forgive again, always able to give man a fresh chance, always able to begin His work again from the chaos of human freedom.

Let us, however, come to the real point. We have been speaking all the time about the world, about man in general. But God's patience is His patience with me. And I to some extent am able to judge what that means. I can judge because I know how difficult it is to be

The Living God

patient with myself. It nearly drives me mad having to bear with myself. Doctors say that it can make man ill and that many mental diseases are caused because man comes to the point where he cannot endure himself any longer and tries to escape from himself by feigning another personality. Often the disease goes even further. It can lead to physical suffering — a curious expiation that man accepts because he cannot overcome the spiritual trouble.

Unless we delude ourselves, or have succeeded in reconciling ourselves to our own paltry and petty world, we all know this kind of suffering, even though it may not have actually made us ill; and, anyway, where is the borderline between health and sickness? We all know the misery, the bitter sterility, when day after day and year after year passes and things never change. One tries for so long to overcome this situation, but it refuses to yield. One appears to have overcome it for a time perhaps, and then it suddenly returns. And sometimes it seems as though after wearing oneself out trying to overcome it, seven demons have taken the place of the original one.[32]

[32] Matt. 12:43-45.

God loves us with patience

If God's attitude toward us is the same as our own attitude toward ourselves, then the outlook is black indeed. If God takes as poor a view of me as I do myself, if God does not bear with my bungling, my dishonesty, and my constant failures with greater patience than I do myself, then I am bound to give up in despair. But God is love. And in Him my nature is truer than in myself. In me it is corrupt; in Him it is pure. In His most holy patience He holds in His love my nature, which I myself disfigure so terribly and squander so thoughtlessly. From this loving patience, He sees and bears me. He has infinite confidence in me. He believes that I am capable of making progress.

We sometimes feel we must get away from ourselves, that we must escape from the old into the new and the real, that sometime or other there must come what the Bible calls conversion, a decisive turning to God. But it does not come, and meanwhile life wastes away. The older we get, the faster it goes and the more difficult we find it to believe that things can ever be any different. Perhaps the greatest thing about God's patience is the infinite possibilities of love and grace that He holds open to life as it hardens in its cowardice and runs on to its end.

The Living God

Can you take this in, this unspeakable, impossible possibility of "hoping against all hope,"[33] which, the more body and soul harden as life ebbs away, must come exclusively from the mind and spirit, from the Holy Spirit of God? This is the ultimate depth of God's patience to which we can pray, that He may keep open for us the possibility of spiritual renewal when all other possibilities have ceased.

One day when Jesus was walking along, He saw a crowd of people. He asked what it was all about, and they took Him through the crowd to show Him an epileptic boy whom the disciples had tried to heal in vain. The father implored Him to help, but Jesus said, "Faithless and misguided generation, how long must I bear with you?"[34]

In the name of Thy charity, do not speak like this, Lord! Surely that is the way we human beings speak. Our life ebbs away, and we get impatient. We reject anything that takes

[33]Cf. Rom. 4:18.
[34]Cf. Mark 9:13-18 (RSV= Mark 9:14-19).

time. But Thou, O Lord, art eternal; Thou hast time. We want everything at once, since we do not know if we shall live to see tomorrow. Thou workest Thy will through the passing ages, and in Thy sight, a thousand years are but as a day. We are foolish and want things to mature before their time; we want to produce things out of their proper time and place. Thou, O God, seest through all things. Thou containest all possibilities in Thyself, and yet Thou art integral and one. Thou art wise and rejoicest that everything occurs in due order. We are sinners, stubborn and disobedient sinners. We are impatient with others because we hate our own wickedness in them. Thou art holy and pure. Thou canst see the evil and yet desire the good. Thou canst wait and allow time for things to mature. Thou canst extract the seed of life from the foulness of decay and make it grow. Thou hast the peace of infinite fulfillment. So, be patient with us, O God. Help us to cling to Thy patience. It is stronger than our bewilderment and sin. If Thou wert to say, "My patience is exhausted," we should be bereft of all hope and power.

8

God reveals His
living presence to us

We have now considered various aspects of the living God; we have discussed various biblical sayings referring to Him. This question may have occurred to you: "How, then, do we come to know Him; how do we become aware of Him?" This is the problem I now propose to investigate.

One thing will be quite clear from the very outset: that we cannot know Him by speculative thought alone. Purely intellectual activity does not lead to a living knowledge of God. It may do good and honest service, but a real awareness of the living God will never be the fruit of mere thinking.

There is, however, such a thing as living thought, the kind that comes from life and returns to life, that interprets life's experiences, brings them into relationship with one another, deepens them, and fits us for new experience. It is the kind of thinking that is sustained, permeated, and directed by all of the faculties of the human spirit — contemplation, conscience, yearning, presentiment, experience of reality, or whatever else one may like to call them. When the heart is ready, the spiritual eye discerns the presence of the Great Other in things and events. Everything points to Him. In Him alone, the lines of life converge — its causes, its wisdom, its yearning, and its purpose. This kind of thinking can indeed lead us to God, and it is this kind of thinking that we are attempting in these talks. May it be really alive, alive in the sight of God!

It is life itself that, permeated by His grace, experiences the living God. But the mind assimilates these experiences of God, organizes, illuminates, and examines them, assesses them, and stands surety for them.

The ways in which this kind of experience and assimilation occur are as various as the spheres of life itself. If we ask great men of faith about their experiences, or if we consider the small experiences that have been granted to us, some of the modes in which the believer becomes aware of the living God will emerge quite clearly.

First of all, there is the experience of conscience. In the course of the day, demands of various kinds are made upon us. Duties require fulfillment, fits of passion have to be overcome, and renunciations must be made. If we fulfill the demands, we have done our duty. If we fail, we know we have sinned. This can happen without our worrying particularly about the ultimate realities behind this moral activity.

One day, however, a duty may confront us with such special significance that we feel that if we come through this particular test, or if we fail, the results will be far-reaching, of more than purely "ethical" importance. The demand that is made on us contains something else. The results of my response to it will have a religious significance. If I fail, something in that sphere will be imperiled and shattered. If I succeed in passing the test, a deep and living holiness will be born in me. This kind of demand is more than an expression of the moral law. It contains the presence of God. And where conscience is open to God, all ethical duty will be seen as a pressure exerted on us by God Himself. The movement of decision that comes from conscience is a movement toward and into God. The action that conscience requires of us is holy, providing an opportunity for God to enter into our lives and win us for His holy kingdom.

Another way in which we can experience God is in the providential dispensations of life. Events of various kinds are taking place around us all the time. People

The Living God

come and go. We have to transact all kinds of business. Events impinge on our lives from many quarters, and the influence they have on us persists and affects other lives. Life is full of this constant interaction; we are constantly influencing and being influenced. For the most part we do not devote much thought to this process. We are content if we come through it unscathed and are able to keep our heads above water and do our work. But sometimes we may feel the presence of something out of the ordinary behind the events that influence our lives. We may feel they are not simply taking place and passing through our lives, but that they have a special relationship to us. The whole thing seems specially intended for us. Some happening may bring a solution or lead to a decision. At some turning point in my life, I may look back and discern a pattern emerging over a long period of time, people and events and circumstances fitting into one another and forming a pattern of life.

It may be objected that this awareness of an evolving pattern is merely a retrospective interpretation imposed on unconnected happenings. It is difficult to answer this objection, since there may be much truth in it. But it does not express the final truth. For all its clarity, the mind behind it sees only half the truth. If we are prepared to open the depths of the heart and the eye of the spirit, a more fundamental truth will appear. We shall see that such patterns do exist after all and that they are brought about not by natural law and dumb necessity, but by a dispensation from another source: by the goodness and wisdom and gentleness and power of grace. This is the experience that Jesus had in mind when He spoke of the "Father in Heaven"[35] and His Providence.

Let us call the organ by which man knows the living God a sense of the pattern of life: the feeling that a fundamental order does exist and a sense of the source from which it comes; and the feeling that fundamentally it is a holy order.

It is possible to have another experience of God: we may know Him as the object of our spiritual yearning. We desire fullness of life, the power of creativity, and the nobility of high standards. We long to be safely enfolded in the depths of love, to be saturated with pure happiness. However one may try to express the object of our yearning, it is always more than any of these descriptions can embrace. This yearning — one might also call

[35] Cf. Matt. 5:16.

it this love that seeks for an object worthy of itself, that seeks for that which can awaken love and satisfy it to the uttermost — searches for means of fulfillment. It asks of many things: "Are you what I am looking for?" And they have to admit they are not. It weighs all things, and ultimately everything is too light. Nothing and no one can satisfy this longing of the soul.

This failure of the soul to find objects and persons worthy of its love may lead to weary renunciation, to a hopelessness that drowns itself in pleasure-seeking, or to a bitterness that turns against everything.

But it may suddenly dawn on the seeker that what he is seeking must nevertheless exist. And it is not only more than the world can give, not only greater or better or more beautiful, but different; unknown and yet familiar; a mystery and yet divined; beyond things and men; on high.

Once this yearning of ours leaves material things behind and reaches out with a pure, searching longing, it has already attained to God. This kind of seeking means that the object of our searching has already been found, for it is the living God Himself who causes us to seek and who uses our restless searching to draw us to Himself.

In such yearning, we become aware of God, even if it may be only in the act of reaching out for Him. God is the object of our longing, and He will satisfy us.

∞

I should like to discuss one last mode of awareness of God. Perhaps it is the most precious of all: the simple knowledge that He is present. It is difficult to talk about this because there is really nothing to be said about it. It is not a question of the nature of God, of whether He has this or that quality, whether He does this or that. All these things are irrelevant here. The all-important thing is that He is present and that He is He.

A comparison may help to show what I mean. I am in the same room as another person to whom I am related by close ties of friendship. I am busy with something or other, and so is he. We don't actually do anything together; we don't talk to one another; we don't even look at one another. Yet I know he is here with me. Permeating all I do or say or think is my awareness that he is here and that he is himself — and the two things are one.

The awareness of God may be of two kinds, empty or full. There may be no sense of another presence — but don't let this apparent contradiction put you off. The heart may feel something is lacking, may sense an emptiness all around it. All is silent. But this emptiness, this silence, has a center to it somewhere. It contains an element of waiting. It is the place of the presence of God. He is present in it because He is absent. The heart is aware of Him because it is aware of His absence. It learns what God is not; it learns that He is not man, that He is not fate, and that He is not a vague sense of the universe.

It is painful but truly blessed to learn what He is not and to feel that He is missing. It may be that after a long period of waiting in absolute quietness, a change will come. There will be something where before there was nothing. It would be wrong to think of this change in terms of a great experience of light or fire or force. We must not throw away what the school of emptiness and silence has taught us. Nothing very special has in fact happened — only that a calm sense of fulfillment has taken the place of the constant sense of emptiness. It is impossible to say what has happened. But He is present with us, and He is Himself.

It is very difficult to name the organ by which this is perceived. The masters of the spiritual life speak of the "apex" or "ground of the soul" or the "spark of the soul," using profound metaphors that have meaning only if what they mean has already been awakened within us.

No doubt there are various other ways of experiencing God. We have considered only a few of them, but these few may open our eyes to the holy and subtle things of the spirit.

The experience of conscience, the experience of Providence, the experience of the yearning soul, and finally the experience of His simple presence: how we come to know God in these various ways, with what faculties, with what part of our being, is almost impossible to say with any exactness.

The right and the devout thing to say is that we are God's creatures. He is He who is and lives. He has created us and permeates us and keeps us. Our createdness is itself, as it were, the "place" that relates us to Him, because it is the place where He, differing from His creatures in His power as Lord and Creator, loves His creatures and enfolds them in His grace.

In the pure and living experience of our createdness, we divine Him who has created us. In the pure and living experience of the finiteness and limitedness of our lives, we divine Him in whom we are, who stands on the other side of our limitations and makes the frontier between Him and us the nearness of His love.

How, I may ask, can it be that I, in spite of the fact that God exists and is all-powerful, do not experience Him more intensely than I experience all other things and more directly than I know myself? The only possible answer is because I am a creature. He is the Infinite One; He is beyond all concepts of measure. He alone can say, "I am who I am."[36] My own finiteness is the veil that hides Him from me. But if I am God's veil — and the very idea is breathtaking — He stands on the other side of my finiteness. It may be objected that it is not only the fact that I am finite that separates me from God, not only the fact that I belong to the world that causes Him who "lives in Heaven"[37] to withdraw into "the inaccessible light,"[38] but also the fact that I am sinful. My sin makes me not merely the veil that hides me from God, but the "darkness" that "comprehendeth Him not."[39] That is certainly true. And yet — and yet I

[36] Exod. 3:14.
[37] Cf. Matt. 6:9.
[38] 1 Tim. 6:16.
[39] John 1:5.

am still His creature and His image in spite of all my sin. Redemption has taken place, and His grace holds sway. And the more absolutely I accept my finiteness, the deeper the humility of my heart, the more honestly I repent my sin — the more it may be granted to me to be mysteriously aware of "the other side."

It is possible that someone will say: "I know nothing of all this. I have a conscience and am aware of its weight, but I think of it only as the ethical imperative, not as the voice of God. I know there is some kind of order in existence, but it is a natural order where nothing happens without a cause. The tangle of events is ordered by the force of life itself and by the self-asserting personality. When something arbitrary or malignant occurs, the life force twists it until it seems a significant woof in a preintended web. No doubt, too, the yearning of which you have spoken exists, but it simply reveals a desire for fulfillment of life. And, in any case, that experience of God's simple presence is quite alien to me. I feel my own existence and that of the things around me; possibly I divine some sort of pattern behind everything, but it is not God."

Such objections must be considered very seriously. To make them honestly is better than to pretend to feel something one does not really possess. But these objections cannot be regarded as final.

The knowledge of God is a living thing. And all living things grow. The Faith teaches us that God exists and that we are capable of knowing him. We must have faith and guard the inner sense of the holy. We must pray for knowledge of God.

Again and again in the Bible we read this: "Unveil my eyes" . . . "open my understanding" . . . "touch my heart"[40] . . . "give me a living heart permeated by the spirit, a heart that can feel."[41] Again and again the Bible refers to the light that is promised to us, in which the reality of God is to be revealed. Again and again it speaks of the nearness of God and of life lived in His nearness; of the face that He will show us and in the sight of which we are to live. And all this is not mere verbiage! These things represent real promises, and they tell us that we can have knowledge of the reality of God. Let us pray for that knowledge. And if the words "Ask and ye shall receive"[42] have any truth at all, then they

[40] Cf. Ps. 118:18, 34, 36 (RSV = Ps. 119:18, 34, 36).
[41] Cf. Ezek. 11:19.
[42] John 16:24.

apply supremely to this gift of gifts: the living knowledge of God.

We must be watchful and alert — on the alert for God. We must take conscience seriously and attend to its depths. We must live our daily life and be ready for it to reveal a pattern and a providence. We must live our lives with people and things and listen for the gentle tokens of God's presence. And for the rest, we must simply wait.

9

All things live for God

The Church's liturgy for the dead contains these words: "Let us worship the King for whom all things live."[43] This is a great conception, that God is He for whom all things live. Nothing that is alive lives far from Him. For Him, nothing dies that is intended to live. Rather, everything that *can* live receives fullness of life in Him.

God is the living God, full of an ineffable power of life. There are various degrees of aliveness. Take a sample number of men and women. They are all alive, or at any rate they are not dead. But in one, life is thin, feeling is meager, and passion is weak. In another, life is ardent, pain is strong, and joy is bright and airy. Whatever happens to the first, he never warms up. Things have no weight; events are colorless. But the other enters into everything. Everything speaks to him;

[43] The author refers to the liturgy as it was prior to the Second Vatican Council. — ED.

everything is radiant and makes an impact on him; everything is instinct with joy or pain.

There are many degrees of aliveness. Sometimes one meets people whose natures are so profound, who have such a capacity for enjoyment, such a gentleness and capacity for suffering, and whose whole being is so involved in the tensions of life, that they make one realize what *life* really means. God is the living God. There is nothing of death in Him. In Him, nothing merely exists: everything is permeated with His life. Nothing is inhibited; everything soars freely in a tense brightness. Nothing is asleep; everything burns in the presence of the one all-embracing life.

So far, we have approached the life of God in human terms. The real aliveness of God is His holiness. That is the deepest foundation of His aliveness, the life revealed in the prophets and in Christ, the life that moves the soul in its authentic encounter with God.

∞

Human beings are born; they grow up; they have their joys and sorrows and their fortunes. They strive and struggle and develop, and all this happens in God. He has created them and given them their various powers. "In Him we live and move and have our be-ing."[44] When we rejoice, the living God is present in our rejoicing. He knows about our joy and rejoices in our rejoicing. And when we suffer, He suffers in our suffer-ing. He has created us, and we are not a matter of indifference to Him.

When we work, it is He who commissions us. It is not a matter of indifference to Him how the carpenter makes the table, how the mother runs her home, and how the doctor serves his patients. There is an inferior kind of piety that seeks to enhance the things of God by disparaging the things of the world. It is the vengeance taken by a frustrated desire for the things of this world.

But the things of the world are not unimportant, nor are they a matter of indifference, least of all to God, since He created the world "that it might be" and He saw that "it was good."[45] He wants it to remain good, and it grieved His heart when sin invaded the goodness of His world. He took that invasion so seriously that He "gave His only-begotten Son."[46] God has put His work

[44] Acts 17:28.
[45] Gen. 1:10.
[46] John 3:16.

into men's hands for them to maintain and continue, and He wants them to complete it for His joy and to give meaning to their own lives. God is with us when we do our work, whatever it may be. We are to do it for Him and with Him.

Human beings meet one another. They touch one another, awaken life in one another, and broaden one another's existence; they contend with one another and grow thereby; they combine with one another in loyalty and love, in the fellowship of life and work — and God is present in all of these relationships. Men and women are His children. He has called them to life. He wants them to grow, one through the other, so that they may "praise Him in greater fullness."[47] The community also lives for God.

He presses in on us in our consciences. Holiness can find room to grow only in freedom. God calls man to give Him room in freedom. When man fails, he is judged by God in his conscience. But the purpose of God's judgment is His desire that man should live. In his sin, man feels that the deepest nerve of real life has been damaged, the nerve of goodness and union with the

[47]Cf. Ps. 108:30 (RSV = Ps. 109:30).

eternal holiness. God makes him feel this. But "He desireth not the death of a sinner but rather that he may turn from his wickedness and live."[48] God does not cut him off. He says: "Thou hast sinned, but there is still a way. The way is different because of sin, but there is still a way. Take thy sin upon thee. Overcome it and then proceed." When man acts rightly, God gives His consent, and there is the bliss of His holy life in this assent. God lives therein, and God's free creatures live and grow in this affirmation.

Through grace, man has been given a share in His own life. Reborn from the depths of God, the believer lives from the divine stream of life, wholly and really himself.

It is a fact that God is alive and all things live for Him. And then comes death.

There is the death that is a consummation. As has been said, in such a death, a man dies his own death. He dies so that his death is, as it were, the fruit of his own most personal life, and so that his life achieves its full

[48] Cf. Ezek. 18:23.

maturity in death. That is a rare grace. But even such a death raises the question: Why must life come to an end at all?

There is also the death that destroys. A young life has come to its flowering: its whole life has been a preparation for the reception of the fullness of life, and it dies. What is the purpose of this sudden rupture? Another person is an indispensable support to other lives, and yet he is suddenly taken away.

Or, one has seen a person growing up, seen his powers developing, seen him acquiring knowledge and attaining self-control, forming a clearer conception of his task in life, gathering experience and approaching what we call mastery. He might have done great things if he had not been torn away all too soon.

All these apparently meaningless deaths are difficult to understand, and even more difficult for the heart to bear. They seem to be a denial of life itself, and to imply a failure on the part of the living God.

∞

Faith tells us that in death God brings life to its true fulfillment. Faith says: whatever shape a human life may take, its span is allotted to it by God, "who desireth not death but life." What He gives to it is its measure, and what may seem to be a rupture is only one form of the span He allots to life. From God's point of view every human being dies his own death, the death that rises from his own life, the death that is intended for him. From the human point of view, death may be a consummation or a sudden break. But at this point we are faced with the mystery of the mind of God.

When a human being dies, he appears before God. Then the veils drop. While man lives, God is everywhere, and yet He is far from man. He is far from man because of what man is. My being and the being of things, although they reflect God and speak of Him, conceal Him from me, make Him inaccessible.

In death this being that hides God from me is shattered. In death there occurs the miraculous irruption of God. God Himself tears the veils away. Death, as our faith sees it, is a grace from God: through it He reveals His presence. In this death man stands before God.

Merely through dying he would not stand "before Him," since no condition whether of life or death is in itself a revelation of God. But God enacts the grace of revealing Himself. Man stands before God, and his whole being flares up like a chip of wood in a vehement fire. Man is kindled into real life. Everything dead in him is burned up.

We living beings are not fully alive. We are weighed down by many of the things we lug around with us. Many things that happen to us merely pass over us. How often we listen to someone telling us his troubles and are desperately aware of our own obtuseness. We are only alive here and there and now and then. But in death everything is compelled into a state of supreme animation, and the lifeless is utterly consumed. All the hardened crusts are burned away, and everything that was constricted breathes in freely.

Guilt is revealed, and repentance becomes immeasurable. But what is Christian repentance? God judges man, and the man who stands before God together with God judges himself. God's holiness is revealed so powerfully and with such ineffable beauty that man measures himself by the standard of God's love — in all things, even in those things in which he has opposed the love of God. He enters into God's judgment against himself with the most ardent passion. And if through God's grace his life was such that despite all its sin his innermost heart was always turned to God, guilt is consumed, and despite its severity, the punishment he takes upon himself is instinct with fervent life. He has penetrated into the life of holiness.

It is said of the dead that "all their works follow after them."[49] What man has done lives on in him. It is part of his living being, strengthening or impeding him. He takes everything with him before God's judgment seat. He enters into the glow of God's presence, and "as if through the fire"[50] in which everything is burned that cannot come alive, he enters into eternal life. Everything from the laborer's hammer blow to the supreme creations of the spirit goes with man and enters into life "as through the fire."

Yet the deepest thing has not yet been said. Through faith, God has implanted a new life in our natural life. It still moves within the natural life, but it comes from Him. It strives to grow into clarity and fullness. But the old life presses down on it, and guilt and despair make it wither, and the violence and weight of finite things conceal it. So it works, underground, comes through here and there, but cannot emerge entirely. One day, however, when man stands before God, it will be revealed

[49] Cf. Rev. 14:13.
[50] 1 Cor. 3:15.

what we are: "the glory of the children of God"[51] will be revealed. Then the inner newness of life will break forth gloriously in the liberating light of God: the early Church called death the day of birth.

God is the King for whom all live.

Eternity is "eternal life." An ancient thinker said that eternal life was the perfect possession, all at once, of never-ending life. But eternal life as understood by the Christian is God; it is the life of God given to man through grace, which he has a share in living.

It has been objected — and it is as well not to ignore such observations — that the idea of eternal life represents a monotonous sameness. But imagine if one were to say to a man the following: "The world is yours: all its materials, its treasures, its dangers, its glories, everything it contains; it is given to you for the joy of your eyes, for your full possession and enjoyment, as a problem for you to solve and an object to conquer. And over and above all this, you are given a mind equal to this measureless gift, a heart strong enough to feel it, a capacity to assimilate it and digest it." Would monotony be possible?

[51] Rom. 8:21.

Eternal life implies that God is given to us as something before which the whole world vanishes into nothingness. And through grace we are given a share in God's own power to see, to love, to judge, to possess, to enjoy. Does the word *monotony*, with its associations, come anywhere near describing the state of eternal life, the fact that eternal life will be an infinite penetration into the infinite wealth of the glory of the living God?

10

*God comforts us as a
mother comforts her child*

On the evening before His death, in the last utterances in which the Lord spoke of His innermost secrets, He gave His disciples this promise: "I will ask the Father and He shall give you another Paraclete, that He may abide with you forever: the spirit of truth; whom the world cannot receive because it seeth Him not; nor knoweth Him; but ye shall know Him, for He shall dwell with you and shall be in you. I will not leave you orphans: [in Him] I will come to you."[52]

We translate the phrase "another Paraclete" as "another comforter." Have you ever considered the meaning of the fact that the spirit of God is called the comforter?

∞

The Church's liturgy contains a wonderful hymn, the sequence for Pentecost. It has the moving quietness

[52] John 14:16-18.

of true holiness and a note of deep inwardness. To understand it, one must become quite still and utterly concentrated; then one will hear its deepest note. It is impossible to convey the calm fervor of the Latin in translation.

Come, Thou holy Paraclete,
And from Thy celestial seat
Send Thy light and brilliancy;
Father of the poor, draw near,
Giver of all gifts, be here;
Come, the soul's true radiancy.

Come, of comforters the best,
Of the soul the sweetest guest,
Come in toil refreshingly;
Thou in labor rest most sweet,
Thou art shadow from the heat,
Comfort in adversity.

O Thou light, most pure and blest,
Shine within the inmost breast
Of Thy faithful company.
Where Thou art not, man hath naught;

Every holy deed and thought
Comes from Thy divinity.

What is soiled, make Thou pure;
What is wounded, work its cure;
What is parched, fructify;
What is rigid, gently bend;
What is frozen, warmly tend;
Straighten what goes erringly.

Fill Thy faithful, who confide
In Thy power to guard and guide,
With Thy sevenfold mystery;
Here Thy Grace and virtue send;
Grant salvation in the end,
And in Heaven felicity.

Amen. Alleluia.

So the hymn moves quietly along, from the heart. It is a gentle dialogue between the heart, with its sufferings and weariness, and God the comforter. The heart knows that every word is heard and answered. The hymn gives us a sense of the meaning of God as the comforter.

The Living God

Man thinks of God as the Mighty One, the Terrible and Threatening One. But His love is nearer to us than the mother to her child, to the child she embraces and for whom she wants only to become a single warm stream of love. The Bible contains this wonderful saying of God: "I will comfort you as a mother comforts her child."[53] He wants to love us with an absolutely under-standing, sympathizing, self-giving love.

Man thinks of God as a stern and lofty challenge, as the relentless Holy One. But He is nearer to us than ever a lover was to his dearest one; He bears in His heart our deepest concerns and bestows on us His ever watchful care. He is devoted to us with the ceaselessly creative trust in the beloved: "Thou art! Thou canst! And I will give thee everything so that thou mayest become what I have implanted in thee."

Man thinks of God as remote and unreal, and this is the worst of all his misconceptions. Power and awful-ness are great things. But it is terrifying to think of God as a pure abstraction, dissolving into nothingness. It is terrifying if all the things around us, houses and trees and people and events, become so real that they oppress

[53] Cf. Isa. 66:13.

126

us and yet He becomes a mere theory, a concept, an insubstantial sound, or a vague atmosphere. Nevertheless, God is real! How near the heart can feel Him! How surely it can experience His awakening and consoling reality! God is the Comforter.

∞

What is the meaning of *comfort*? How does it come about?

Certainly not by reasoning and reckoning. Advice and argument are no comfort: they leave us cold. They leave man alone in his need and suffering. Nothing comes to him from them. But comfort is full of life; it has an immediacy and an intimacy that make all things new.

To comfort, you must love. You must be open and enter into the other's heart. You must be observant; you must have the free and sensitive heart that finds the paths of life with quiet assurance; you must be able to discover the sore and withered places. You must have the subtlety and strength to penetrate to the living center, to the deep source of life that has dried up. The heart must combine with this source of life, must summon it to life again so that it can flow through all the deserts and ruins within. To do this is truly to comfort.

The Living God

To do this is to awaken, to generate, and to create. To do this is to call forth the best in the other person. Such comfort liberates in the very act of permeating. It releases, supports, and broadens, but in such a way that the other rises again from his own true center and makes a fresh beginning.

A person who has been wounded is comforted when someone who loves him awakens the hidden energy within him so that it passes through the wound in a healing stream. A person who is spiritually dried up is comforted when someone who loves him releases the wave of life within and everything is revived. A person who has lost things of great value, who has had his work destroyed and his hopes dashed, is comforted when someone who loves him allies himself with something that lies at a deeper level, underneath the individual possession and the individual work; allies himself with the fundamental creative will, and rouses it to new activity; allies himself with that innermost soul that is above change and loss and is the eternal strength of the heart; admitting the loss that is lost in time, but winning it anew from the timelessness of faith in God. A person whose heart is sullied is comforted when someone who loves him is able to touch the purity that lives below the sin, and rouse a new confidence in his ability to overcome the ugliness of his heart. A person who has sinned and can find no escape from his troubled conscience is comforted when someone who loves him is able, without the slightest presumption, to shed light on the sinner's self-deception, to release and fortify the will and open up new ways and possibilities. There is comfort when the lover is able to soften the hardened, to touch the paralyzed with relaxing warmth, to give a new direction to an erring mind.

Human love, really pure and selfless human love, is able to comfort. But it soon attains its limits. Human love is not the love of God.

Christ sent us the One who is "the nearness"[54] between the Father and the Son: the Holy Spirit. He is the holy inwardness of God Himself; in the secret language of love He is the "tie," the "kiss." In Him God has come to us as the Comforter.

The Holy Spirit is nearness. He is the nearness of the holy — the nearness of the unapproachable. He is the

[54]Cf. 2 Cor. 13:13 (RSV = 2 Cor. 13:14).

inner being of the inaccessible. He is the holiness whose very breath is love. He "searches out the depths of the Godhead."[55]

He has come to us to be in us, so that we may learn from Him how to utter the name of Jesus, how to pray, and how to profess our faith. He has come to us and in us, that we may be renewed and born again in Him. He holds the roots of our lives in His hands. He is the Creator creating from the freedom of the pure fullness of love. He is able to console.

The hopelessness all around us is endless; its bitter fullness is inexhaustible, as manifold as all the life that has fallen away from the heart of God: the hopelessness of the suffering that wounds and tires, of the narrowness that constricts our sight and breathing, of the yearning that pines away, of the unalleviated pain, of the tormenting sin, and of the weakness that is powerless to rise again. The hopelessness of the dreariness when the heart knows no joy and no pain; when the days are empty and silent and everything that happens is meaningless; when one knows what life would be like if one could only love but cannot love, and when one's soul

[55] Cf. 1 Cor. 2:10.

thirsts within and goes about as in a barren and dry land — is there any power sufficient to overcome this power?

There is a saying: "Send forth Thy Spirit and all things will be created and Thou shalt renew the face of the earth."[56] Do you realize that that is true — that He can come like a gentle breath "blowing where it listeth and thou hearest the sound thereof but canst not tell whence it cometh, and whither it goeth,"[57] and that He can touch your soul and make everything different? What was real before still remains, yet everything has been renewed. Then you become aware that you have a heart and that you, too, have received the ability to love, and things are filled with a gentle and holy meaning, and you know that everything is good and that it is worthwhile — divinely worthwhile — to be alive and to persevere.

It is when this happens to us — and the Lord promised that it would happen to us when He promised us the Comforter — that we realize the meaning of true comfort.

[56]Ps. 103:30 (RSV = Ps. 104:30).
[57]John 3:8.

The Living God

∞

There is a phrase in the hymn we have quoted that contains the most subtle secret of this comfort. After the gentle petitions "Father of the poor, draw near, Giver of all gifts, be here," we sing, "Come, the soul's true radiancy" or, literally, "Come, Thou light of all hearts." A holy mystery lies hidden here, waiting to teach us the wonder of this "light of all hearts."

We know that there is a light of the eyes; at any rate, we imagine we know what is meant by that: the light that comes from the sun or from a lamp when it is lit. We also understand what is meant by the light of the mind: we have an inkling of its meaning when an idea suddenly dawns on us. But "the light of the heart" — what does it signify? It is a great mystery that light shines from the center of the emotions, that the nearness and being of the beloved beams with light, that the heart with its love is not blind, but endowed with sight, that the brightness of the spirit and of knowledge is not cool and does not merely shine from afar, but is glowing and full of the immediacy and intimacy of the close at hand.

Behold, this is the comfort of God: the guide that leads us through confusion, the warmth that loosens our frost and frigidity, the power that heals, and the renewer of purity and beauty.

∞

One more thing, and the most important of all: this hymn that seems to have sprung from the remotest stillness is full of daily life with its burdens, noise, and troubles. That is a real comfort. The comfort of which we have spoken extends to all the forces that mold our daily lives. There is a healing presence in the midst of daily labor, a cooling breeze in the heat and burden of the day, a spring of consolation in the midst of suffering and sorrow. This comfort is so real that it will not dry up in the withering torments of life, so vital that it cannot be stifled by any weariness. It is the comfort of the living God.

11

God will create for us
a new Heaven and earth

We have already spoken of the mysterious life that comes to man from the love of God, "from above,"[58] from Heaven, which is given to him and which is yet his very own and which makes him what he is most truly intended to be. But what about all the things around us? Does this mystery of new life apply only to man? Does it not touch all the things of the wide, rich world: the nobly towering mountains, the trees in the abundance and mystery of their quiet life, the beautiful stars, the immense forces of the universe, the impenetrable depths of the world, testifying so mightily to their own existence? All the great and precious things around us — do they have no part in the mystery of God's freely given life? Does this life extend only to man?

Some people feel that there is a deep expectation in nature, that there is more in nature than material things that can be touched and used. In fairy tales there is a

[58] John 3:31.

137

hint of a universal mystery in nature, of a yearning and the wonder of its fulfillment. Are these intimations purely fanciful, or do they presage a reality?

We read in the letter to the Romans: "For the expectation of the creature waiteth for the manifestation of the sons of God. For the creature was made subject to vanity, not willingly, but by reason of Him who hath subjected the same in hope: because the creature itself also shall be delivered from the bondage of corruption into the glorious liberty of the children of God. For we know that the whole creation groaneth and travaileth in pain together until now."[59] This is a strange passage. It appears to imply that the world is not yet complete, that it yearns to be completed and is travailing to attain this goal, that something is struggling to develop that is powerless to do so in its own strength, and that its emergence is bound up with the "revelation of the glory of the children of God." What does this mean?

∞

Have you ever noticed how a child treats things? The things around him seem to come alive. When a

[59]Rom. 8:19-22.

child takes things into his heart and hands, they acquire a strange freedom. They mean much more than they do to us adults. They have quite a different depth. Something behind them is released. They confide in one another. A form that is normally hidden appears, and this is the real thing. Things speak; they are on intimate terms with one another and with the child; they become friendly and attractive and strong and dangerous in quite a different way.

But then the child grows older, and this relationship to things fades away. The child grows up and becomes rational; he wants to use things, to control and enjoy them, and they lose the freedom that they had when he was a child. They are imprisoned. They fall silent. They shrivel up. Occasionally the mystery emerges again, in the spring perhaps, when everything is stirring with new life, or in the hovering darkness of the night.

There are adults who seem to have a similar influence on the things around them but on a higher plane. St. Francis of Assisi[60] was one such person. The reports of how he called the fishes and preached to them, how

---

[60]St. Francis of Assisi (c. 1182-1226), the founder of the Franciscan order.

he spoke to the birds about the glory of God, and how the wolf of Gubbio heard and obeyed his warnings are no doubt legendary, but it is significant that such legends should have been woven around a man at all. It means that this Francis of Assisi was one in whose presence things were different from what they are in the presence of ordinary human beings. In his presence they acquired a new nature. They were released from their dumbness, their fetters fell away from them, and stunted things blossomed and became beautiful, free, and noble. More than that, something entirely new was awakened in them.

This was not a fairy tale, but a miracle — not in the usual sense, but in the sense that in the presence of this true child of God and his conspicuously blessed "glory," something from God entered into them; and this was what they had been waiting for, longingly and painfully; something in which their innermost spirit was fulfilled and in which they were enabled to be wholly themselves for the first time.

This was what people felt, and in order to express what they felt, they produced these legends about St. Francis. What St. Paul had in mind began to be true: "The creature was made subject to vanity, not willingly, but by reason of Him who hath subjected the same in hope: because the creature itself also shall be delivered from the bondage of corruption into the glorious liberty of the children of God." This glorious liberty of the children of God began to be revealed in St. Francis and around him. In his presence the world began to be redeemed. In his eyes and his heart and hands, things began to be different. This is a mystery full of great promise.

And if we open the last book of the Bible, the book of the secret revelation, we find that it speaks of the sufferings in the world undergone by the holy life that comes from God and of the struggles in which it must persevere; but at the same time, it speaks of the glory that God will cause to radiate from the whole of creation. The whole book of Revelation is filled with the deep mystery of the love of God, not only for man, but for things. That God loves things as well as loving man is at the very heart of the Christian Faith. The sun, the stars, the trees, all finite things, all of them, silent and soulless: God loves them with a special love.

It is very good to note the passages in the Bible where this truth shines forth. At the beginning of the Old Testament, in the story of how God created the world, we read, "And He saw that it was good."[61] A smile of God's love passes over the beauty of His creatures.

And the sentence also contains a defense of His world. When it was written, there were people who said the world was evil since it came from the Evil One: it had been created by an evil force. But the Bible says: No, what God has created is good, very good. "And God saw everything He had made, and behold it was very good."[62] The Bible constantly speaks of sin, of the corruption and suffering that have come into the world and into things because of sin, and of the delusion and temptation that lie in the things of the world. But the world is never given up in despair. God always holds it in His hands. It is His world. In spite of all the destruction, it still bears the marks and the image of God in its order and in a thousand forms, and it speaks of its Creator to those who come to it devoutly and with purified hearts.

Jesus Himself looks on it with a kindly eye. His parables are alive with flowers and birds, fields and vineyards. He has revealed to us that the great mystery

[61] Cf. Gen. 1:10.
[62] Gen. 1:31.

of the Father's Providence is accomplished in the events of this world, that the things of this world are the instruments and vessels of His Providence and intimations to His children of His goodness. He has made the spring of eternal life rise from the things of the world, the water of Baptism, the bread and wine of the Last Supper.

St. Paul says that the existence and the rule of the invisible God can be seen from the visible life of material things.[63] And in profound imagery he proclaims the mystery of the world that waits and yearns to be born again. All these things are signs that God values the things of this world, that He loves them and loves them dearly. This mystery shines forth in all its radiance in the last book of the Bible, Revelation. There the glory of God's love flows through all things, most profoundly of all in the wonderful phrase "a new Heaven and a new earth"[64] in which all pain and all oppression and hatred will be no more, and all the "former things" and everything that stems from sin will pass away.[65] Everything

[63] Rom. 1:20.
[64] Rev. 21:1.
[65] Cf. Rev. 21:4.

will be free. Everything will be open. Everything will be changed.

The Resurrection of the Lord — and what took place earlier on the Mount of Transfiguration[66] — reveals the glowing, divine center of this transformation. The body of the Lord was transfigured as the outward expression of His inner glory. But the transfigured Lord is alive. He lives and acts. He draws the world unto Himself. He wants to transform it into the single great mystery of His own mystical transfigured body; not only the human race but all creatures, so that "everything that is in Heaven and on earth and under the earth may be summed up in Him as the Head,"[67] all creation a unity, permeated by the power of His divine-human life. All life! All light! Everything one in the beauty of love!

How inspiringly Revelation speaks of all this! Vision after vision rises before us: the noise of a great multitude, like the noise of water in flood, or the noise of deep thunder;[68] choirs of figures in white robes and golden crowns prostrate and adoring; immense multitudes of

[66] Matt. 17:1-2.
[67] Cf. Col. 1:16-18.
[68] Rev. 19:6.

singers praising God;[69] towering lamps burning before the high throne standing on gold and crystal and sapphire;[70] the heavenly city: its walls made of precious stones, its twelve gates twelve single pearls, one pearl for each gate, and the street of the city of pure gold like transparent glass[71] — an excess of glory, which the writer strives to convey in words that stagger the imagination.

There is no need of sun or moon, for the Lamb is the light thereof and the light of God flows through it. Its food is the fruit of the tree of eternal life, which grows by the pure river of the water of life.[72]

These are images, parables of the beauty that is to break forth from the whole creation in the transformation brought about by God, when the glory of the children of God has been revealed. It is that beauty which is the delight of God, from which, as Revelation proclaims, the Holy City will descend and go forth like a bride to meet the Lamb.[73]

[69] Rev. 4:4; 7:11.
[70] Cf. Rev. 4:5-6.
[71] Rev. 21:21.
[72] Rev. 21:23; 22:1-2.
[73] Cf. Rev. 21:2; 19:7.

The Living God

Sometimes in the late afternoon, when the day has been very clear, an hour comes when the air is utterly pure and everything seems transparent. A gentle and powerful beauty reigns over all, an earthly image of "the new Heaven and the new earth." It seems to transfigure all things. But such earthly beauty is a mere promise of things to come. One day the light of God's heart will break forth from all things, and they will be radiant, and the meaning of God's love for His creation will be revealed to us.

Romano Guardini

(1885-1968)

Although he was born in Verona, Italy, Romano Guardini grew up in Mainz, Germany, where his father was serving as Italian consul. Since his education and formation were German, he decided to remain in Germany as an adult.

After studying chemistry and economics as a youth, Guardini turned to theology and was ordained to the priesthood in 1910. From 1923 to 1939 (when he was expelled by the Nazis), Msgr. Guardini occupied a chair created for him at the University of Berlin as "professor for the philosophy of religion and Catholic *Weltanschauung*." After the war, similar positions were created for him, first at the University of Tübingen and then at the University of Munich (1948-1963).

Msgr. Guardini's extremely popular courses in these universities won him a reputation as one of Germany's most remarkable and successful Catholic educators. As a teacher, writer, and speaker, he was notable for being able to detect and nurture those elements of spirituality that nourish all that is best in the life of Christians.

After the war, Msgr. Guardini's influence grew to be enormous, not only through his university positions, but also through the inspiration and guidance he gave to the postwar German Catholic youth movement, which enlivened the faith of countless young people.

Msgr. Guardini's writings include works on meditation, education, literature, philosophy, theology, and art. Among his many books, perhaps the most famous is *The Lord,* which has been continuously in print in many languages since its first publication in 1937. Even today, countless readers continue to be transformed by these beautiful books, which combine a profound thirst for God with depth of thought and a delightful perfection of expression.

The works of Msgr. Guardini are indispensable reading for all Christians who want to remain true to the Faith and to grow holy in our age of skepticism and corrosive doubt.

Sophia Institute is a nonprofit institution that seeks to restore man's knowledge of eternal truth, including man's knowledge of his own nature, his relation to other persons, and his relation to God.

Sophia Institute Press® serves this end in numerous ways. We publish translations of foreign works to make them accessible for the first time to English-speaking readers. We bring back into print books that have been long out of print. And we publish important new books that fulfill the ideals of Sophia Institute. These books afford readers a rich source of the enduring wisdom of mankind.

Sophia Institute Press® makes these books of high quality available to the general public by using advanced technology and by soliciting donations to subsidize our general publishing costs.

Your generosity can help us provide the public with editions of works containing the enduring wisdom of the ages. Please send your tax-deductible contribution to the address below.

The members of the Editorial Board of Sophia Institute Press® welcome questions, comments, and suggestions from all our readers.

For your free catalog, call:
Toll-free: 1-800-888-9344

or write:
Sophia Institute Press®
Box 5284
Manchester, NH 03108

Internet users may visit our website at
http://www.sophiainstitute.com